30-SECOND
RELIGION

30-SECOND
RELIGION

The 50 most thought-provoking
religious beliefs, each explained
in half a minute

Editor
Russell Re Manning

Contributors
Richard Bartholomew
Mathew Guest
Graham Harvey
Russell Re Manning
Alexander Studholme

Illustrations
Ivan Hissey

METRO BOOKS
New York

METRO BOOKS
New York

An Imprint of Sterling Publishing Co., Inc.
1166 Avenue of the Americas
New York, NY 10036

ISBN: 978-1-4351-3003-6

For information about custom editions, special sales, and premium and corporate purchases, please contact Sterling Special Sales at 800-805-5489 or specialsales@ sterlingpublishing.com.

Manufactured in China

10 9 8 7 6

www.sterlingpublishing.com

Credits:
Creative Director **Peter Bridgewater**
Publisher **Jason Hook**
Editorial Director **Caroline Earle**
Art Director **Michael Whitehead**
Designer **Ginny Zeal**
Concept Design **Linda Becker**
Profiles Text **Nic Compton**
Glossaries Text **Nic Compton**
Assistant Editor **Jamie Pumfrey**

CONTENTS

INTRODUCTION
Russell Re Manning

Religion is back. Of course, for millions of believers around the world it never really went away. Notwithstanding the confident predictions of 20th-century advocates of secularization, nor indeed the more aggressive declarations of the so-called "new atheists" of the 21st century, religious beliefs and practices continue to thrive. And no wonder—they are so fascinating, diverse, and intriguing.

This book is not about "religion"—surely no convincing single unified definition could ever suffice—but about religions. More precisely, it is about 50 prominent religions that between them span the spiritual life of the world—from ancient traditions with origins that have been lost in the mists of time and mythology to brand new religious movements.

Perhaps the most striking thing about religions is the dramatic variety of the beliefs and practices of the faithful. Religions are not monolithic institutions, but living communities of believers. While this makes them fascinating to study, the variety of religious beliefs and spiritual practices can make them a daunting prospect for the interested "lay person." Religious beliefs and practices can seem confusing to the uninitiated, the language used can be specialized and obscure, and the finer points of doctrinal debate can seem frankly about as relevant as the apocryphal medieval question about the number of angels able to dance on a pinhead. Fortunately, this book can help. In the pages that follow, the 50 key religions are summed up in plain English—no jargon and no waffle. The central beliefs and distinctive features of each religion are set out

Rich variety

Religion has been a part of everyday life for many cultures since antiquity. From major religions to less widespread sects, this book explores the diversity and symbolism of the world's religions.

accessibly and engagingly in less than the time it takes to offer a prayer. Each 30-second religion is presented alongside a single-sentence 3-second sermon for those in the spiritual fast lane, while for those taking the contemplative path, the 3-minute theology delves that bit deeper into the mysteries of the faiths.

The religions are organized into seven chapters. The first, **Indigenous Religions**, includes some of the oldest religions in the world, mostly closely related to particular cultures. In the second, **Eastern Spiritualities**, the major religious traditions of Asia are surveyed, while the third, **Abrahamic Traditions**, covers those traditions historically anchored in the Middle East that share a common lineage to Abraham. The next two chapters deal with the varieties of the world's most widespread religion: **European Christianities** treats those Christian denominations with historical roots in Europe, while **World Christianities** includes Christian churches with origins outside Europe. **Fusion Religions** focuses on those religions that combine elements from different traditions to create religious fusions and the final group, **New Religions**, introduces some of the major new religious movements of the 20th century. Along the way, we stop off at the seven key sacred texts, taking a look at some of the most profound and influential books of all time.

This book can be read it two ways. If you read it cover to cover—from Genesis to Revelation—you will get an excellent overview of the dazzling diversity of religions and the rich variety of their beliefs and practices. Otherwise, dip into individual entries here and there; you'll be surprised at some of the connections between religions. Go on, seek enlightenment!

Sacred texts

Throughout the centuries, the key tenets of many religious traditions have been passed down through sacred texts—many of which remain in use to this day.

אָנֹכִי

יְהֹוָה

לֹא

תִשָּׂא

לֹא

כַּבֵּד

וَإِذْ أَخَذْنَا مِيثَاقَكُمْ لَا تَسْفِكُونَ دِمَاءَكُمْ وَلَا تُخْرِجُونَ

أَنْفُسَكُمْ مِنْ دِيَارِكُمْ ثُمَّ أَقْرَرْتُمْ وَأَنْتُمْ تَشْهَدُونَ ۝

ثُمَّ أَنْتُمْ هَؤُلَاءِ تَقْتُلُونَ أَنْفُسَكُمْ وَتُخْرِجُونَ فَرِيقًا

مِنْكُمْ مِنْ دِيَارِهِمْ تَظَاهَرُونَ عَلَيْهِمْ بِالْإِثْمِ وَالْعُدْوَانِ

وَإِنْ يَأْتُوكُمْ أُسَارَى تُفَادُوهُمْ وَهُوَ مُحَرَّمٌ عَلَيْكُمْ

إِخْرَاجُهُمْ أَفَتُؤْمِنُونَ بِبَعْضِ الْكِتَابِ وَتَكْفُرُونَ بِبَعْضٍ

فَمَا جَزَاءُ مَنْ يَفْعَلُ ذَلِكَ مِنْكُمْ إِلَّا خِزْيٌ فِي الْحَيَاةِ الدُّنْيَا

وَيَوْمَ الْقِيَامَةِ يُرَدُّونَ إِلَى أَشَدِّ الْعَذَابِ وَمَا اللَّهُ بِغَافِلٍ

हरे हरे राम हरे हरे हरे

हरे हरे

بِالْآخِرَةِ فَلَا يُخَفَّفُ عَنْهُمُ الْعَذَابُ وَلَا هُمْ يُنْصَرُونَ

وَلَقَدْ آتَيْنَا مُوسَى الْكِتَابَ وَقَفَّيْنَا مِنْ بَعْدِهِ بِالرُّسُلِ

وَآتَيْنَا عِيسَى ابْنَ مَرْيَمَ الْبَيِّنَاتِ وَأَيَّدْنَاهُ بِرُوحِ الْقُدُسِ

أَفَكُلَّمَا جَاءَكُمْ رَسُولٌ بِمَا لَا تَهْوَى أَنْفُسُكُمُ اسْتَكْبَرْتُمْ

فَفَرِيقًا كَذَّبْتُمْ وَفَرِيقًا تَقْتُلُونَ ۝ وَقَالُوا قُلُوبُنَا

غُلْفٌ بَلْ لَعَنَهُمُ اللَّهُ بِكُفْرِهِمْ فَقَلِيلًا مَا يُؤْمِنُونَ ۝

神道

INDIGENOUS TRADITIONS

cosmos The universe, but particularly from the ancient Greeks' perspective of the universe as a harmonious whole—from the Greek word *cosmos*, meaning "order." The ancient Greeks saw the universe as completely interconnected and achieving a natural balance, similar to the view proposed today by the Gaia environmental movement.

devotee An enthusiastic, and possibly fanatic, follower of a religion. Not all followers of a religion are necessarily "devotees," which comes from the Latin word *devotus*, or "faithful." A more neutral term is "follower" or "adherent."

deity A god or other holy or sacred being. Most deities are the spiritual manifestation of a particular characteristic or life force, such as Ganesha, patron of science and learning in Hinduism, and Apollo, god of music in ancient Greece.

diaspora The spread of a people or culture from their ancestral home. Thus the diaspora of a religion is the multiple manifestations of that faith in various geographical locations. Spelled with a capital "D," it is usually interpreted as referring specifically to the migration of Jews from Israel. From the Greek *diaspeirein*, "to scatter seed."

divination A method of foretelling the future either by reading specially designed artifacts, such as tarot cards and rune stones, or interpreting omens in everyday life. Other forms of divination include: astrology, palmistry, crystal gazing, Chinese throwing sticks, and inspecting the entrails of a slaughtered animal. Most modern established religions, such as Christianity and Islam, condemn the practice.

indigenous Belonging to the locality where it is found; not imported from elsewhere. Most indigenous religions have developed over millennia and are closely entwined with the region's ecology.

medium A person who is said to contact the spirits of the dead and other paranormal forces and to act as an intermediary with the living. Contact is usually made when the medium falls into a trance and allows the spirit to use his or her body to communicate either verbally or through writing or other signs. The practice is prevalent in certain religions, such as Spiritualism and Voodooism.

metaphysical Relating to metaphysics, that is the study of the essential nature of being, including fundamental scientific truths and the spiritual dimension. The word is derived from the Greek words *metá* (meaning "beyond" or "after") and *physiká* (meaning "physical"). The main areas of modern metaphysics are: ontology (the nature of being), natural theology (the existence of God), and universal science (essential scientific principles).

monotheism The belief that there is only one God, as opposed to polytheism (many gods) and pantheism (God within nature). Judaism, Christianity, and Islam are prominent monotheistic faiths. From the Greek words *mono* ("single" or "alone") and *theos* ("God").

peyote A rounded, green cactus from Mexico from which the hallucinogenic alkaloid mescaline can be extracted. Use of peyote, also known as mescal button, is said to induce psychedelic trances and other out-of-body experiences. The plant has been used in religious rites and for medicinal purposes by Mexican tribes for over 3,000 years. Today, the Native American Church practices Peyotism.

polytheism The belief in more than one God. Most polytheistic faiths worship a number of deities, each of which represents different aspects of nature or the human character. These are used to explain the creation of the world and other natural phenomena. Most modern religions are polytheistic, including Hinduism, Confucianism, Taoism, and most African religions.

shaman A holy man or woman who acts as a medium or conduit between the physical world and the spiritual world. Shamans claim to channel supernatural forces to cure ailments and even control the weather. Although the term originates from Siberia, they are prevalent in most tribal cultures, especially Native American tribes.

talisman A piece of jewelry or other small object that is thought to possess magical properties and endow its wearer with special powers or to protect them from harm. The configuration of the stars when a talisman is created is sometimes said to invest it with a magical charge.

YORUBA

the 30-second religion

Yoruba traditional religion has

many similarities with other African traditional religions, including the ways in which it has creatively fused with other religions in the global Yoruba diaspora. People honor and seek the aid of one or more of the *orishas* (deities) and ancestors (those who have died but remain interested in their descendents) to support attempts to live fulfilled, healthy, and respectful lives. Many Yoruba believe in a "high God," Olodumare, above the many *orishas*, perhaps manifest *as* the many *orishas*. For them, Olodumare is the creator who started everything, but generally leaves the running of the earth to the *orishas*, each of whom is linked with specific phenomena. Shango, for example, is associated with lightning and electricity. In this fusion of animism and polytheism, deities exist in a rich web of relationships in a thoroughly social universe. A creative energy called "ashe" flows through everything. Public and private rituals, including sacrifices, are conducted to celebrate and enhance these relationships, which are expected to benefit the devotees as well as the deities or ancestors, especially by the sharing of "ashe." Religious knowledge is conveyed through divination systems, empowering stories, traditional practices, and dramatic festivals often involving masks and drums.

RELATED RELIGIONS
See also
ANIMISM
Page 18
ABRAHAMIC TRADITIONS
Pages 56–77
EUROPEAN CHRISTIANITIES
Pages 78–97

30-SECOND TEXT
Graham Harvey

3-SECOND SERMON
Yoruba traditional religion is a vibrant way of seeking inspiration and energy from deities, ancestors, and other beings so that people can live fulfilled lives.

3-MINUTE THEOLOGY
The belief in a "high God," Olodumare, almost certainly originates from contact with Christians and Muslims. However, it should not be dismissed as a foreign import but celebrated as evidence of the vitality of a religion strong enough to also re-enchant modern processes, such as electricity generation and car making. In diaspora, Yoruba religious creativity is evident in Caribbean religions such as Santería, which fuses tradition with Roman Catholic Christianity, so that the *orishas* share costumes and feast days with "saints."

Drawing on the traditional past while embracing the present, Yoruba celebrates health, respect, and fulfillment.

ABORIGINAL DREAMING

the 30-second religion

30-SECOND TEXT
Graham Harvey

For Australian Aborigines, the Dreaming is the foundation of Law (rules) and Lore (teachings, often in the form of story, dance, or art) for living—it shapes how things are and should be. The Dreaming is also a fundamental aspect of creation. Before life, there was a dark, flat, featureless land. Beneath it existed (and will always exist) all possibilities. Occasionally, elements erupted through the surface, creating hills, valleys, rivers, and springs, even bringing forth sunlight. The elements were the ancestral forms of humans, kangaroos, bees, dingoes, and all life. As they traveled over the land, they created areas known as "countries." An ancestral caterpillar drops food, for example, and creates scrubland. Two dingoes fight, leaving pieces of flesh to become rocks. The ancestral forms interacted together: dancing, painting, sharing, and marrying. The ancestors then returned beneath the newly formed land surface, and their descendants (ordinary humans, kangaroos, bees, and dingoes) began to inhabit the land, following the lifestyles and rules established for them by their ancestral forms—the most important ones are those that require all inhabitants of countries to bear mutual responsibility for the well-being of that living community.

3-SECOND SERMON
The Dreaming is the continual formation of all life—together with rules for living—out of a preexisting chaos of fertile potential.

3-MINUTE THEOLOGY
The Dreaming is often presented as a collection of "just-so" stories about "creation-time." It is, in fact, a complex summary of the rights and responsibilities people have for dwelling cooperatively, without overconsumption, in specific regions. Its expression in art (from traditional rock art and body adornment to contemporary acrylics) and music (from funerary didgeridoo playing to urban fusions) now has global recognition. The Dreaming bears influence in legal land-rights cases as well as religious initiation rituals.

The Dreaming is a potent mix of creation myth and ancestral lore dating back thousands of years, and has at its heart a message of responsibility.

ANIMISM

the 30-second religion

Animism is not in itself a religion,
but as a belief system, is present in a number of
religions. It refers to the worldviews of many
indigenous people and some Pagans. In
Animism, "persons" does not mean human or
humanlike, but members of a multispecies
community, perhaps including "rock persons"
and "hedgehog persons." Adherents of animist
religions claim to know that at least some rocks,
animals, or plants are persons because they
give and receive gifts, engage in conversations,
or seem to act toward others intentionally.
Humans, too, are only "persons" because they
act in these ways. To respect other persons
does not necessarily mean liking them. It
means acknowledging they also have rights
and interests. Persons can be killed, but only
when necessary and always compassionately.
Animist religions often feature shamans: experts
in resolving interspecies misunderstandings
(such as when humans insult hunted animals),
knowing the whereabouts of others (such as
distant food species), or combating aggressors
(such as disease persons). Their work often
involves dramatic trance rituals. Generally,
animism is expressed in simple gift-giving to
other persons, as when Native Americans offer
tobacco or sage to elders or sacred beings.

RELATED RELIGIONS
See also
YORUBA
Page 14
MESOAMERICAN RELIGION
Page 22
SHINTO
Page 54

3-SECOND BIOGRAPHIES
DANIEL QUINN
1935–

DAVID ABRAM
1957–

30-SECOND TEXT
Graham Harvey

3-SECOND SERMON
Animism is a way of seeing
the world—including
animate and inanimate
objects—as a community
of living "persons," all
of which deserve respect.

3-MINUTE THEOLOGY
Animist beliefs play a
key role in evolutionary
explanations of religion.
Some cognitive and
evolutionary psychologists
theorize that a belief in,
for example, thunder
and lightning being a
manifestation of an
angry spirit is "minimally
counterintuitive," in
that it fulfills intuitive
assumptions while
violating some of those
assumptions in a small
way. Such beliefs are
attention grabbing and
memorable and, thus,
provide the basis for most
religious convictions, as
well as potentially being
useful evolutionary
adaptions.

*It's not just humans
who have feelings,
animals, plants, and
rocks do, too—they
all deserve respect.*

NATIVE AMERICAN CHURCH

the 30-second religion

Religious consumption of peyote cactus bulbs originated in remote antiquity among indigenous peoples in what is now Mexico. It spread northward rapidly from the 1880s, becoming a vital spiritual source in many reservation communities. Significant quantities (chewed or prepared in a tea) induce powerful visions, inspiring the founders and leaders ("roadmen") of the Native American Church (NAC), but milder brews heighten people's awareness and enable them to focus on concerns beyond their everyday troubles. Peyote is consumed sacramentally, not recreationally, because it is understood to come from the Creator's heart to bring healing, knowledge, and the motivation people need to lead healthy and moral lives. The NAC is the largest peyotist movement. Legally incorporated in the United States in 1918, it arose from the teachings of prophets, such as John Wilson and John Rave, who experienced peyote as a healer and guide, and who encouraged a fusion of indigenous and Christian practices. Jesus and the Bible, for example, are important to many NAC members. Indigenous traditional protocols blend local and continent-wide practices to make variations in NAC rituals and address specific communities' needs. The NAC encourages respect for the earth and the use of "natural" products.

3-SECOND SERMON
The Native American Church (NAC) is a pan-Native American religion that is best known for the use of peyote as a sacrament.

3-MINUTE THEOLOGY
The Native American Church or "Peyote Road" encourages sobriety, family care, self-reliance, and the unity of Native peoples. In addition to nightlong vigils that inspire unity, the NAC is respected for the antialcohol effects of peyote consumption and of its teaching. Legal struggles against the criminalization of peyote as a "drug" have led to freedom of religion laws that permit its sacramental use, including among Native Americans in U.S. prisons. NAC often works alongside indigenous traditionalists.

3-SECOND BIOGRAPHIES
QUANAH PARKER
1852–1911

JOHN RAVE
1856–1917

JOHN WILSON
1860–1901

JAMES MOONEY
1861–1921

30-SECOND TEXT
Graham Harvey

For NAC members, the hallucinogenic property of the peyote cactus is an essential source of profound spiritual inspiration.

MESOAMERICAN RELIGION

the 30-second religion

RELATED RELIGIONS
See also
ANIMISM
Page 18

30-SECOND TEXT
Graham Harvey

3-SECOND SERMON
Mesoamerica (from central Mexico to northwest Costa Rica) is typified by similar religions in which humans participate with other beings to keep the cosmos working.

3-MINUTE THEOLOGY
After the Spanish invasion, a tension between a single culture and local differences remains clear in various forms of Latin American Christianity, which often include elements from pre-Columbian traditions. Regional festivals and dance ceremonies are evidence of fusions between Catholicism and Mayan or other cultures. Pre-Christian pilgrimages continue by including saints among those addressed in prayers—and those expected to reciprocate by enhancing the well-being of the devout.

Prior to the Spanish conquest, a broad, common religious culture existed across Mesoamerica. Trade, similar language traits, and especially a reliance on corn agriculture by settled populations, with some large urban centers, unified the region. Over time and distance, significant diversity is also evident. Large, centralized empires (such as that of some Mayan groups) contrast with smaller societies, influencing spiritual diversity. From the civic rituals of urban centers to the shamanic healing rituals of villages, people sought to maintain harmony, such as by offering blood to enable deities to control cosmic processes, recording astronomical observations to maintain auspicious timing, or expressing gratitude to corn for its sacrificial gift of life. Purification ceremonies aided respectful relationships with nonhuman persons of these animist and polytheistic communities. Should, for example, someone drop corn on the ground, rituals apologized for the unintended insult to this sacred plant person. Temple complexes and pottery illustrate the religiously expressive art of the region, because they are often adorned with divine and shamanic beings. Dramatic polarities, such as night and day, male and female, and conflict and harmony, for example, could result in tension but were important in the continuous regeneration of life promoted by religious activities.

A common thread running through Mesoamerican religion was a desire to keep the cosmos in balance—sometimes involving human bloodletting.

SHENISM

the 30-second religion

Shenism identifies the shifting creative fusions of a distinctively Chinese-style spirituality. It shares many properties with traditional Chinese medicine, and popular religious activities often make use of dominant Buddhist, Confucian, and/or Taoist ideas, practices, officials, and locations. People visit shrines and temples, seek the ritual services of priests and monks, and make use of sacred texts and talismans. Whether or not people identify as members of the more organized forms of those religions can be contentious. The localized and kinship foundation of much of Chinese popular spirituality gives it a place among indigenous religions. This is particularly true when Shenism involves mediums to communicate with ancestors (named members of a family who, although dead, are still deemed to be interested in their descendants' well-being), and the use of divination. The word *shen* has a wide range of meanings, perhaps illustrated by the similar potential of one of its English translations, "spirit." Both words might refer to metaphysical entities (ancestors, ghosts, local deities, or beings who speak through mediums), or they might also refer to states of consciousness and refined internal energies, suggesting practices of focusing attention, meditation, trance, or seeking health and fulfillment.

RELATED RELIGIONS
See also
MAINSTREAM BUDDHISM
Page 36

TAOISM
Page 48

CONFUCIANISM
Page 50

30-SECOND TEXT
Graham Harvey

3-SECOND SERMON
Shenism is a recent label for the varieties of popular religious practices in China that draw on, but are not officially involved in, Buddhism, Confucianism, or Taoism.

3-MINUTE THEOLOGY
A tension between "worldly" interests (seeking personal and family health, wealth, and harmony) and "other-worldly" interests (pursuing beneficial reciprocal relationships with ancestors and deities, and well-being for ancestors and oneself in future states, such as in heaven or in rebirth) is crucial to the relationship between Shenism and more organized religions. There are few official practices and teachings concerning such matters, but popular or democratic desires, needs, and fears encourage the self-taught feel and diversity of Shenism.

Shenism—the worship of shens (deities or spirits)—is a collection of Chinese folk religions influenced by Buddhist, Confucian, and Taoist principles.

ZOROASTRIANISM

the 30-second religion

Around 3,000 years ago an Iranian prophet, now known as Zarathushtra (or Zoroaster following Greek pronunciation), is said by Zoroastrians (or Parsis in India) to have initiated the religion's emphasis on "good thoughts, good words, good deeds." A cosmic struggle between good and evil not only confronts humans as the context of all existence, but takes place in the everyday moral choices that each person has to make. Some Zoroastrians emphasize the moral struggle as the key teaching—the freedom of choice between good and evil. The struggle involves the eternal Wise Lord, Ahura Mazda, in opposition to a destructive adversary, Ahriman. A number of other beings, the Beneficial Immortals, are present in the constituent elements of the cosmos and in the struggle. Rather than pollute earth, water, or fire, Zoroastrians traditionally exposed their dead on high towers, where vultures consumed their flesh. By combating "bad thoughts, bad words, bad deeds," Zoroastrians work toward the purification and proper ordering of the cosmos. Rituals led by priests, individual action, and community life are guided by a variety of sacred texts—such as the *Gathas*, a series of hymns that encourage vigilance against all negative thoughts or acts.

RELATED RELIGIONS
See also
ABRAHAMIC TRADITIONS
Pages 56–77
EUROPEAN CHRISTIANITIES
Pages 78–97

3-SECOND BIOGRAPHIES
ZARATHUSHTRA (ZOROASTER)
fl. c. 5000 BCE

DARIUS 1
c. 558–486 BCE

30-SECOND TEXT
Graham Harvey

3-SECOND SERMON
Probably the oldest living religion, Zoroastrianism identifies the struggle between good and evil as the context of all existence.

3-MINUTE THEOLOGY
Zoroastrian philosophical influence on the theologies and cosmologies of monotheistic religions was foundational. Relatively small populations of Zoroastrians survive now, primarily in Iran and India. Variations in practice occur, such as in the timing of Nav Ruz, the new year festival, celebrated at spring equinox in Iran to symbolize the victory of light over darkness, but in August in India because Parsis there have not adjusted their calendars for leap years.

Ancient and mystical, Zoroastrianism is as much philosophy as it is religion—with the struggle between good and evil, order and chaos at its core.

AHMADIYYA

the 30-second religion

3-SECOND SERMON

The Ahmadiyya is a revivalist movement within Islam, which breaks from Islamic orthodoxy in its adherence to the teachings of a messianic leader.

3-MINUTE THEOLOGY

The Ahmadiyya movement has a fervent global missionary program that seeks the promotion of Islam through peaceful means, especially the propagation of literature and translation of the Qur'an into numerous languages. In this sense, the movement stresses the interpretation of jihad as primarily a struggle against one's own base desires. Following Ahmad's teaching, the concept of violent jihad (holy war) is viewed as unnecessary in modern times—the right response to hate being love and kindness.

The Ahmadiyya movement was founded in India in 1889 by Mirza Ghulam Ahmad, who believed himself to be the promised Messiah, or Mahdi, for the Muslim community. At various times, Ahmad also claimed to be the Mujaddid, or "renewer," of Islam, an avatar of the Hindu god Krishna, the returned Jesus, and a manifestation of the Prophet Muhammad. While consistently maintaining that a chief goal is to revitalize Islam, Ahmadis are generally viewed as suspect by orthodox Muslims. While Ahmad maintained that he was subordinate to Muhammad, his claim to deliver a new revelation of God's teaching, intended to return Islam to its proper state, sat uncomfortably with Islam's central tenet that Muhammad is the "seal" of the prophets. Indeed, this has led to some persecution of the Ahmadiyya in Muslim countries, such as Pakistan, in which it has been declared a "non-Muslim minority." Ahmadis retain a primary place for the teaching of Ahmad alongside the Qur'an, and this includes a call for the end of religious wars and the institution of peace and social justice. Like the Baha'i, Ahmadis recognize the teachings of other religious founders, including Zoroaster, Buddha, and Confucius, but Ahmad taught that these converge in the one true Islam.

3-SECOND BIOGRAPHIES

MIRZA GHULAM AHMAD
1835–1908

MAULANA HAKEEM
NOOR-UD-DIN
1841–1914

MUHAMMAD ABDUS SALAM
1926–1996

30 SECOND TEXT
Mathew Guest

Often shunned by orthodox Muslims, the Ahmadiyya community are supporters of the self-proclaimed Messiah and prophet Mirza Ghulam Ahmad.

BAHA'I FAITH

the 30-second religion

Baha'ism originated in Iran in the 1860s as a movement within Babism, which in turn was a sect within Shi'a Islam. Its founder, Bahá'u'lláh, believed himself to be a prophet with a new set of revelations, conceived as emerging within a long line of successive prophets including Abraham and Jesus. Originally confined to the Middle East, Baha'ism expanded into the United States in 1894, and found the religious diversity there well suited to its ambitions to break away from Shi'a Islam altogether—instead proclaiming itself as a new world faith, at once the successor and culmination of all world religions. Baha'is are distinctive in remaining committed to its global mission (especially in the developing world), while affirming radically inclusive values, including the oneness of humanity, universal education, the harmony of religion and science, monogamy, and equality of the sexes. The movement also exists without a strict hierarchy or priesthood, although it has a rationalized administrative structure and views Bahá'u'lláh and his writings as manifestations of divinity. Baha'is gather together on a local basis for prayer, sacred readings, and for shared food and communal activities organized by locally elected assemblies.

3-SECOND SERMON

Central to Baha'ism is a conviction of the essential unity of all religious faiths, reflecting its emphasis on celebrating humanity and seeking world peace.

3-MINUTE THEOLOGY

While it has its theological roots firmly in 19th-century Iranian Shi'a Islam, Baha'ism has been most radically shaped over the past 100 years by its encounter with Western culture. Expanding through the West, it has developed ideals of global unity that dovetail with values associated with transnational organizations, such as the United Nations. However, the Baha'i vision of unity is not based on democracy as such, but on what it sees as universal principles of morality.

RELATED RELIGIONS
See also
SHI'A ISLAM
Page 68

3-SECOND BIOGRAPHIES
BAHÁ'U'LLÁH
1817–1892

'ABD AL-BAHA
1844–1921

SHOGHI EFFENDI
1897–1957

30-SECOND TEXT
Mathew Guest

Expanding from its Shi'a Islam ancestry, Baha'ism promotes itself as a global faith with religious unity, world peace, and equality at its core.

EUROPEAN CHRISTIANITIES

Assumption The taking of Mary's body to heaven after her death, also known as the Dormition (falling asleep). Celebrated by Roman Catholics for hundreds of year, with the feast of the Assumption on August 15, it was only made part of Catholic dogma by Pope Pius XII in 1950.

elect According to Calvinism, those preselected by God for salvation.

Eucharist A Christian ceremony that commemorates the meal Christ shared with his disciples before being crucified. The Last Supper is reenacted through drinking wine (or grape juice) and eating bread. Although all Christians celebrate the Eucharist, they differ in their interpretation of it, with Catholics believing the bread and wine are the actual body and blood of Christ, while Protestants take a less literal approach.

evangelical Belonging to a form of Christianity that seeks to return to the basic tenets of the New Testament, instead of later interpretations. The movement started with the teachings of Martin Luther, John Calvin, and Ulrich Zwingli in the 16th century but has since been adopted by many other fundamentalist churches.

excommunicated To be excluded from a church or religious community.

Fall, The In Christian mythology, this is the moment humankind lost its innocence and committed its first sin. Despite being told by God not to eat the fruit from the Tree of Knowledge, Adam and Eve succumb to temptation, whereupon they become ashamed of their nakedness and are expelled from paradise.

First Great Awakening A revival of religious piety that took place in the Americas in the mid-18th century. The movement was inspired by powerful evangelical sermons by charismatic preachers, which appealed to people's personal guilt. Starting in Pennsylvania and New Jersey, the movement was spread throughout the Americas by missionaries. The Second Great Awakening was a similar movement that took place in the early 19th century.

Gospel The first books of the New Testament, named after Jesus' followers Matthew, Mark, Luke, and John, traditionally considered to be their authors. Gospel also refers to Jesus' message, or the "good news" of salvation. The word itself comes from the Old English *godspel*, meaning "good tidings."

Great Schism The splitting of the Christian Church into the Roman Catholic and Greek Orthodox factions in 1054 (also known as the East–West Schism). The separation occurred for a number of reasons, including the refusal of the Greek-speaking Catholics to recognize Rome as the primary authority for their faith. There was also disagreement about the formation of the Holy Spirit and whether the bread at communion should be leaven or unleaven.

icons Figures or paintings of sacred figures, such as Christian saints, venerated in certain religions.

Immaculate Conception The idea that Mary, mother of Christ, was conceived without sin. This is different from the virgin birth, which suggests that Mary gave birth to Christ while remaining a virgin throughout.

indulgence The forgiving of a sin and remission from punishment. In the Middle Ages, indulgences were given out by the Catholic Church as a reward for good deeds and devout behavior. However, the system was increasingly abused, with professional "pardoners" raising funds for the Church (and themselves) through the sale of indulgences.

predestination The theory that God has decided the outcome of all things into infinity, including who will be saved. Calvinists extend the idea further and believe in "double-predestination," that God has predetermined who will be saved and who will be left to suffer eternal damnation for their sins.

Reformation A movement in 16th-century Europe that attempted to reform the Catholic Church and rid it of corrupt practices, such as the sale of indulgences. It began with the publication of Martin Luther's *The Ninety-Five Theses* in 1517, and lead to the dissolutions of monasteries in England and the creation of the Protestant churches.

sacrament A religious ceremony thought to bestow a blessing on those who take part. The Protestant Church recognizes two sacraments, baptism and Holy Communion, while the Catholic Church has seven: baptism, confirmation, confession, marriage, ordination, Holy Communion, and Last Rites.

Tree of Knowledge A tree in the Garden of Eden from which Adam and Eve were forbidden to eat. Their failure to obey God's word was, according to Christian belief, humanity's original sin.

ROMAN CATHOLICISM

the 30-second religion

3-SECOND SERMON
The largest Christian denomination, headed by the Pope and with a mission to spread the good news (Gospel) of Jesus Christ, administer the sacraments, and exercise charity.

3-MINUTE THEOLOGY
For Catholics, Jesus' mother, Mary, is a figure of widespread popular veneration. Catholics believe Mary was conceived without sin ("Immaculate Conception"), that she herself conceived Jesus miraculously through the agency of the Holy Spirit ("virgin birth"), and that at the end of her earthly life she was taken up to heaven body and soul ("Assumption"). Many important Catholic shrines are associated with miraculous appearances of Mary, notably, at Guadalupe, Fatima, and Lourdes.

The Roman Catholic Church is the largest unified religious organization in the world—over half the world's Christians are Catholics. The head of the Church is the Bishop of Rome (known as the Pope from the informal Greek term *pappas* for "father"), who claims unbroken succession from Saint Peter, the first Bishop of Rome and designated leader of Jesus' followers. The Catholic Church considers its primary purpose is to proclaim the good news (Gospel) of Jesus Christ, namely that God has saved the world from its state of sin by becoming incarnate in the man Jesus of Nazareth. For Catholics, the Church itself is the continuing presence on earth of Jesus, ensuring that God's work of salvation is maintained until Jesus' prophesized return. Sacraments are central to the Catholic Church's work, understood as visible signs of God's grace entrusted to the Church. The principal sacrament is the Eucharist, in which bread and wine are believed to be transformed into Jesus' body and blood. Catholics believe that after death each person's soul is judged: the virtuous unite with God in heaven; the wicked are separated from God in hell; the rest find purgatory, a temporary state of cleansing before admission to heaven.

RELATED RELIGIONS
See also
ABRAHAMIC TRADITIONS
Pages 56–77
EUROPEAN CHRISTIANITIES
Pages 78–97
WORLD CHRISTIANITIES
Pages 98–115

3-SECOND BIOGRAPHIES
JESUS
C.5 BCE– C.30 CE

SAINT PETER
C.1 BCE– 67 CE

THOMAS AQUINAS
1225–1274

30-SECOND TEXT
Russell Re Manning

Mary plays a much more significant role in Catholicism than in any other Christian Church—the image of the Madonna and Child is notably widespread.

MORMONISM

the 30-second religion

The Church of Jesus Christ of

Latter-day Saints was founded by Joseph Smith in 1830 in Fayette, New York. Mormons believe that Smith received a series of religious visions in which he was given specific instructions and authority to restore the Christian Church. Central to these was the unearthing and translation of a holy book written on plates of gold and containing the story of God's dealings with the ancient people of the Americas, as compiled by the ancient American prophet Mormon. Mormons use this book alongside the Christian Bible (in the Authorized King James Version) in religious teaching and study. Mormons believe in the continuation of prophecy: living prophets are chosen by God to act as means through which revelations can be communicated. For Mormons, all people can receive inspiration from God, but in practice God uses senior Church officials. For Mormons, Jesus is the first-born son of God and the only perfect human being and they believe that by following his example, they might achieve salvation, or the gift of an eternal life with God. Unlike many Christians, Mormons do not believe in original sin, but assert that each individual sins by choosing to do wrong. Hence salvation, while enabled by God's grace, requires the performance of good actions in imitation of Jesus.

RELATED RELIGIONS
See also
ORTHODOX JUDAISM
Page 60
EUROPEAN CHRISTIANITIES
Pages 78–97
WORLD CHRISTIANITIES
Pages 98–115

3-SECOND BIOGRAPHIES
BRIGHAM YOUNG
1801–1877

JOSEPH SMITH
1805–1844

30-SECOND TEXT
Russell Re Manning

3-SECOND SERMON
The Church of Jesus Christ of Latter-day Saints that aims to restore Christianity with new revelations of God's acts and nature.

3-MINUTE THEOLOGY
In contrast to many Christians, Mormons do not believe that God created the universe out of nothing (*ex nihilo*), but that God—the all-powerful and all-knowing supreme being—created it out of preexisting material, which he ordered into its proper forms. For Mormons, God has a physical body (albeit exalted in heaven), Jesus is the perfect first-born son of God, and the Trinity consists of three distinct beings united in a common purpose.

The Book of Mormon,
as translated by Joseph Smith from golden plates, forms the basis of Mormon doctrine and is considered the most "correct text."

JEHOVAH'S WITNESSES

the 30-second religion

The Jehovah's Witnesses is the largest and best known of a group of millenarian restorationist Christian denominations that emerged out of the Bible Student Movement of the late 19th century, founded by Charles Taze Russell. Through continuous preaching and the journal *Zion's Watch Tower and Herald of Christ's Presence*, Russell critiqued many of the established Christian doctrines and taught the urgent message that the second coming of Christ was at hand. Through a mixture of literal and symbolic interpretations of the Bible, Jehovah's Witnesses believe in Russell's predications of the imminent apocalypse—including a cosmic battle between the forces of heaven and the forces of Satan—and the Rapture (assumption into heaven) of all true believers. Jehovah's Witnesses interpret political events, as well as the evidence of global climate change, as proof that the world is coming to an end. Unlike many Christians, Jehovah's Witnesses do not believe in the Holy Trinity, believing God (or "Jehovah" after God's original Biblical name, the Tetragrammaton JHVH, or YHWH) to be Universal Sovereign, Jesus to be God's only direct creation, and the Holy Spirit to be God's power in the world. Jehovah's Witnesses also believe Satan to be a fallen angel, who, along with his demons, misleads people and causes evil and human suffering.

3-SECOND SERMON
The last days began in 1914, leading to the imminent destruction of the world by God's intervention and the deliverance of those who worship Jehovah.

3-MINUTE THEOLOGY
Evangelism is central to Jehovah's Witnesses, in particular, the practice of spreading their beliefs by visiting people's homes. The *Watchtower* commentaries and other teaching material are widely available, with some texts translated into over 500 different languages. Jehovah's Witnesses use and distribute a new translation of the Bible, the *New World Translation of the Holy Scriptures*, of which over 165 million copies have been published in over 80 languages.

RELATED RELIGIONS
See also
ORTHODOX JUDAISM
Page 60
EUROPEAN CHRISTIANITIES
Pages 78–97
WORLD CHRISTIANITIES
Pages 98–115

3-SECOND BIOGRAPHIES
JESUS
C.5 BCE–C.30 CE
CHARLES TAZE RUSSELL
1852–1916

30-SECOND TEXT
Russell Re Manning

Jehovah's Witnesses believe Russell's prediction that Armageddon will cleanse the earth, and God will create a paradise that will be ruled over by Jesus Christ and 144,000 of the anointed.

BAPTIST CHRISTIANITY

the 30-second religion

A diverse group of Christian denominations, Baptists take their name from their practice of adult baptism. Unlike most Christians, who baptize infants or young children into the fellowship of the community of Christians (known as "infant baptism, or pedobaptism"), Baptists insist that individual believers freely and publically commit themselves to their Christian faith in a ceremony of adult baptism (known as "believers' baptism," or "credobaptism"). Often these baptisms are full immersions, in which the believer is lowered completely beneath the surface of the water, emerging in the eyes of the Church as "born again" in Christ. Baptist churches emerged in the early 17th century within various Protestant denominations, and, while today there is still no central Baptist authority, two prominent confederations are the Baptist World Alliance (BWA) and the Southern Baptist Convention (SBC). In 2004, the SBC, the largest Protestant denomination in the United States with over 16 million members, voted to leave the BWA over fears of a drift toward theological liberalism. Generally evangelical, Baptists require that the New Testament be the explicit authority for their beliefs and practices. While not always taking the Bible literally, Baptists insist that Christian beliefs and practices are commanded or commended by example within the Bible.

3-SECOND SERMON
Baptism of adult believers is an outward sign of repentance of sins and confession of faith in Jesus Christ as the Son of God.

3-MINUTE THEOLOGY
Baptists believe that religious faith is a matter of a personal relation between God and the believer. This support for "religious freedom" entails that individuals may practice any religion, or none. Historically, they have been ardent supporters of the principle of the separation of Church and State, particularly in the United States. Of course, Baptists have the evangelical hope that individuals will confess a Christian faith, but insist that this must be a free decision.

RELATED RELIGIONS
See also
ORTHODOX JUDAISM
Page 60
EUROPEAN CHRISTIANITIES
Pages 78–97
WORLD CHRISTIANITIES
Pages 98–115

3-SECOND BIOGRAPHIES
JESUS
C.5 BCE–C.30 CE
JOHN SMYTH
C.1570–C.1612
THOMAS HELWYS
C.1575–C.1616
ROGER WILLIAMS
C.1603–1683

30-SECOND TEXT
Russell Re Manning

For Baptists, only adults can profess to a true faith in Jesus Christ and repent of their sins.

SEVENTH-DAY ADVENTIST CHURCH

the 30-second religion

3-SECOND SERMON
A Christian community that observes the Sabbath on Saturday and which is preparing for the imminent return of Jesus Christ.

3-MINUTE THEOLOGY
Seventh-day Adventists believe in so-called "investigative judgment." This is generally meant as an interpretation of Daniel 7:10 and Revelation 20:12, which talk of the opening of the "book of life," in which all the deeds of humanity are written. According to these visions, Satan accuses believers of transgression and unbelief and Jesus acts as advocate, whose atoning sacrifice helps to blot out believers' sins. Those whose names remain are punished by permanent destruction.

Formally established in 1863, the Seventh-day Adventist Church is the largest and most significant Christian Church to have emerged from the Adventist movement of the 1840s, when the imminent "Second Advent" of Jesus Christ was predicted. When this did not happen (known as "the Great Disappointment"), the predictions were reinterpreted to suggest that Christ had entered "the Most Holy Place" of the heavenly sanctuary and that the process of divine judgment had begun. Seventh-day Adventists also believe that the Bible commands Christians to observe the "Sabbath"—that is to keep Saturday (not Sunday) as a day of rest and worship. No secular work may be performed; instead, the day consists of worship, charitable work, and family orientated activities, such as nature walks. Even secular recreational activities, such as competitive sports, are generally avoided. Influenced by the writings of Ellen G. White, Seventh-day Adventists place considerable emphasis on Christian deportment, ranging from sexual ethics of abstinence and strict dietary observance to conservative attitudes toward dress and leisure activities. Although it may not appeal to some, the sober Adventist lifestyle seems to be good for the health: a recent study claims that male Adventist Californians live 7.3 years longer than their non-Adventist neighbors!

RELATED RELIGIONS
See also
EUROPEAN CHRISTIANITIES
Pages 78–97
WORLD CHRISTIANITIES
Pages 98–115

3-SECOND BIOGRAPHIES
JESUS
C.5 BCE–C.30 CE

WILLIAM MILLER
1782–1849

ELLEN G. WHITE
1827–1915

JOHN HARVEY KELLOGG
1852–1943

30-SECOND TEXT
Russell Re Manning

A healthy body and a healthy soul—Adventists emphasize health through abstinence from alcohol, tobacco, and often meat.

CHRISTIAN SCIENCE

the 30-second religion

In 1875, Mary Baker Eddy
published a book entitled *Science and Health with Key to the Scriptures*. Eddy, who had been experiencing persistent health problems for many years, tells of how in 1866 she had recovered unexpectedly from a bad fall and had founded the new religion of Christian Science. In 1879, the First Church of Christ, Scientist was founded in Boston, Massachusetts. Central to Christian Science is the belief that prayer can lead to healing and, in most cases, should be preferred to conventional medical treatment. This is not, however, because God is thought to intervene miraculously in the world. Instead, Christian Scientists believe the material world to be a distorted version of the true world—a world of spiritual ideas. Prayer enables an undistorted vision of the spiritual reality. Illness is understood to be the result of a mistaken conviction in the reality of a material problem; hence, healing is the removal of this error by the recognition that the problem is only really an illusion. Christian Scientists regard Jesus Christ as the "Wayshower" and consider his healing "miracles" as exemplars of his spiritual understanding: an understanding that is available to all humanity.

3-MINUTE THEOLOGY
For Christian Scientists, the relation between Christian belief and the natural sciences is simple. The natural sciences describe the unreal world of the material and as such are illusory; instead Christian Science leads to an understanding of the real immortal world of spiritual ideas. There is no real conflict: the natural scientific accounts of biological evolution are as mistaken as "Creationist" accounts: both come from the belief in the reality of the material world.

RELATED RELIGIONS
See also
EUROPEAN CHRISTIANITIES
Pages 78–97
WORLD CHRISTIANITIES
Pages 98–115

3-SECOND BIOGRAPHIES
JESUS
C.5 BCE–C.30 CE

MARY BAKER EDDY
1821–1910

30-SECOND TEXT
Russell Re Manning

God encompasses the spiritual reality, which is truth and good. According to Christian Scientists, the material world, including evil, is unreal and false.

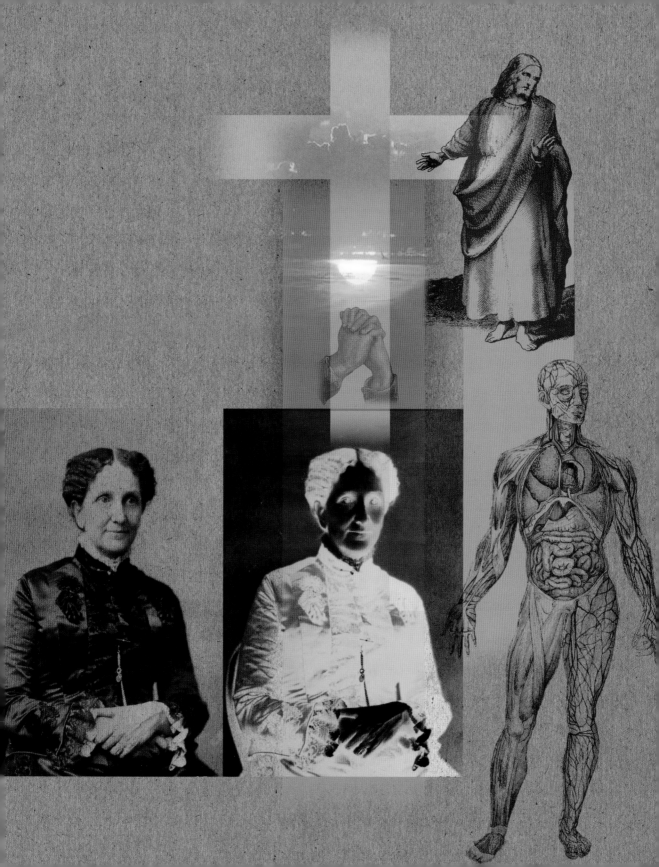

FUSION RELIGIONS

animal sacrifice The ritual killing of an animal to appease or petition deities. It is sometimes interpreted as the killing of humankind's baser, "animal" instincts, or simply as sacrificing something precious to prove devotion. Many religions practice animal sacrifice, including Hinduism, and there are numerous descriptions of it in the Old Testament.

Bhagavad Gita A section of the Mahabharata, composed in c.250 BCE, in which Krishna reveals himself to Arjuna and embarks on a long theological discussion about human nature and the meaning of life. Many of the central tenets of Hinduism are discussed, including the dissolution of ego and following the natural path.

black magic The channeling of malevolent spirits and other paranormal phenomena to create spells and bring about evil deeds, or the belief that this is possible.

Christian spiritualists People who combine their Christian faith with spiritualist beliefs. The main attraction for such people is the alleged ability to contact the dead and communicate with their loved ones. Orthodox Christian religions maintain that the Bible expressly forbids contacts with the dead, quoting passages from Deuteronomy (18:11) and Luke (16:19–31).

ectoplasm A substance said to exude from various orifices, or possibly the pores, of mediums while they are in a trance. Starting as a smoke or vapor, it is said to react to light and turn into a clothlike substance.

medium A person who is said to contact the spirits of the dead and other paranormal forces and to act as an intermediary with the living. Contact is usually made when the medium falls into a trance and allows the spirit to use his or her body to communicate either verbally or through writing or other signs. The practice is prevalent in certain religions, such as Spiritualism and Voodooism.

Odin In Norse mythology, the supreme God, who created heaven, earth, and the first human beings, Ask and Embla. He was also venerated as the god of poetry, wisdom, knowledge, magic, prophecy, war, hunting, victory, and death.

pantheon A temple devoted to the gods, such as the building of that name in Rome, or a collective name for a group of gods or deities.

paranormal Something that cannot be explained by normal experience or currently accepted scientific laws. Typical examples are telepathy, divination, astrology, channeling, ghosts, and UFOs.

Satanists Those who worship Satan. The term is sometimes used by Christian fundamentalists to describe all non-Christians. The real Church of Satan, however, has well-defined principles, such as fulfilling desires and not turning the other cheek, but also being kind to those who deserve it and not harming children.

séance A meeting of people, usually around a table, to contact the spirits of the dead. A medium is usually used as an intermediary, and messages are relayed in the form of speech, writing, cards, or Ouija boards. From the French meaning "to be seated," originally it referred to any meeting but especially meetings of the legislature.

shamanism The belief that the world is filled with spirits, which can be influenced by a holy man. The shaman is thought to be able to heal people and resolve problems within communities by connecting with the spirit world and restoring balance. The religion is prevalent in Asia and Siberia and among Native American tribes.

spirit The nonphysical, metaphysical part of a person; their essential life force. Many religions consider that it is the spirit that gives the body life, and that the spirit survives after the body has died.

syncretism The merging of different faiths, usually implying a successful new fusion. Christian Spiritualism is one example. The Baha'i faith, which accepts Muhammad, Jesus, Moses, Buddha, Zoroaster, and Abraham as prophets, is considered another, although it has its own prophet, Bahá'u'lláh, and its own holy scriptures.

Wicca A pagan or nature-based religion that is said to have its roots in pre-Christian witchcraft. Covens of Wiccans use magic rituals to celebrate seasonal festivals based around a Mother Goddess. Some claim sexual acts are involved.

zombie A dead body brought to life by supernatural forces. In Voodoo religions, the term can also refer to a spell cast to bring a corpse back to life and control it. The concept originates in West Africa but has been popularized in Western popular culture through novels and movies.

NEO-PAGANISM
the 30-second religion

Neo-Pagans are inspired by the ancient pre-Christian religions of Europe (and, to a lesser extent, the Middle East), and there is a diversity of beliefs and emphases. Hellenic Neo-Pagans, for example, worship Greek deities, such as Zeus, while others look to Norse gods, such as Odin. The best-known strand, however, is known as Wicca, which stresses the notion of a Goddess of fertility and rebirth, and her male consort, the Horned God of the forests. Nature is to be respected and celebrated—both in the rhythm of the year and the life cycle—and humans in harmony with nature can become adepts of "the Craft," the use of magic. However, such self-described "witches" are cautioned to use magic for healing and for personal development instead of for outward manipulation. Some Neo-Pagans regard the deities as real beings, others as symbolic representations of natural forces and aspects of human characteristics. Much of the scholarship on "the Goddess" that Wicca draws on is today regarded as historically problematic, but members are often aware of this and are willing to regard such texts as "founding myths."

RELATED RELIGION
See also
ANIMISM
Page 18

3-SECOND BIOGRAPHIES
GERALD GARDNER
1884–1964

ALEX SANDERS
1926–1988

MAXINE SANDERS
1946–

STARHAWK
1951–

30-SECOND TEXT
Richard Bartholomew

3-SECOND SERMON
Humans should live in harmony with nature by venerating ancient gods and goddesses, while magical rituals can bring healing and spiritual growth.

3-MINUTE THEOLOGY
With its stress on a female divinity and its empowering reclamation of the label "witch," Wicca in particular has attracted some feminist support. However, because the Goddess is often portrayed as a stereotypically alluring, slim young woman, the movement has been critiqued for entrenching gender essentialism. Neo-Pagan practices—particularly those that involve nudity—are regarded with hostility by many Christians, and Wiccans have often complained of being accused of Satanism by churches and the media.

Neo-Paganism is an essentially polytheistic, religion, recognizing a divine Goddess, and celebrating nature as a divinity in its own right.

5.

SPIRITUALISM

the 30-second religion

Spiritualists believe that mediums can convey messages from the spirit world. Communications may be religious teachings from a spirit guide, or personal messages from deceased loved ones. A spirit may communicate in various ways: the medium may go into a trance and either speak the spirit's words or write them down—if the medium is consulted during a séance, in which a small group of people sit around a table, the spirit may answer by rapping on the table or by tipping it. Alternatively, the medium may stand before a larger audience and claim to receive personal information from a variety of spirits about particular people present. Some mediums advertise themselves as able to provide messages for people who contact them by telephone or text message; in the past, some claimed that during their trance their bodies would exude ectoplasm, a substance that would form into the image of the spirit and which could be photographed. Despite the Biblical taboo against contacting the dead, there are Christian Spiritualists, some of whom emphasize teachings received from a disciple of Jesus called Zodiac. The spirit world is thought to consist of various levels or "spheres"; spiritual progression continues after death.

3-SECOND SERMON
The dead can communicate from the spirit world with the living via mediums, providing information and other manifestations that scientifically prove life after death.

3-MINUTE THEOLOGY
Spiritualism claims to offer scientific evidence for the afterlife, in the form of information that the medium could not have known without communication with spirits. As such, it has attracted considerable interest from investigators of paranormal phenomena, some of whom have become convinced that mediumship is genuine. Others, however, believe that, due to wishful thinking, those who consult mediums overlook incorrect information and the medium's ability to coax or discern information naturally.

3-SECOND BIOGRAPHIES
EMANUEL SWEDENBORG
1688–1772

MARGARET FOX
1833–1893

LEONORA PIPER
1857–1950

ARTHUR CONAN DOYLE
1859–1930

DORIS STOKES
1920–1987

30-SECOND TEXT
Richard Bartholomew

Spiritualists believe that the spirit survives death. Messages from the spirit world are relayed to the living via mediums.

VOODOO

the 30-second religion

According to the beliefs of

Voodoo, there are thousands of spirits (*lwa*) that interact with humanity. These *lwa* were once human, and they are classified into "nations" that reflect the ancestral homelands of African slaves. Some spirits are generous *rada* spirits, while others are more aggressive *petro* spirits, although these can be seen as alternative manifestations of the same *lwa*. Certain spirits are particularly associated with the dead; these are the *gede*, headed by Baron Samdi and known for their trickery and raucous behavior. The spirits were all created by the Supreme God, Bondye, who considers petitions from humans conveyed by the *lwa* but who is otherwise uninvolved with humanity. The *lwa* are served by Voodoo priests (*oungan*) and priestesses (*manbo*), and contact with the *lwa* can occur through dreams, possession trances, or divination. Rituals include drumming and dancing, because these attract the spirits and induce possession, while animal sacrifice provides the spirits with sustenance. There are also malign lesser spirits, *baka*, who can be manipulated for selfish purposes by sorcerers, called *boko*. *Boko* are also thought to have the power to create zombies; these are bodies controlled by the *boko* by capture of the owner's soul.

RELATED RELIGIONS
See also
YORUBA
Page 14
CANDOMBLÉ
Page 126

3-SECOND BIOGRAPHIES
BOUKMAN DUTTY
d. c.1791

MARIE LAVEAU
1794–1881

MAYA DEREN
1917–1961

30-SECOND TEXT
Richard Bartholomew

3-SECOND SERMON
Many spirits make themselves known through dreams, trances, and communication with priests; Voodoo rituals provide healing, assistance, and protection from evil forces.

3-MINUTE THEOLOGY
Many followers of Voodoo consider themselves to be Roman Catholics, despite the Church's antagonistic attitude toward the religion. Many of the *lwa* are identified with Roman Catholic saints—such is the gatekeeper *lwa* Legba; he is often associated with Saint Peter, who in Catholic tradition holds the keys to heaven. Some Voodoo practitioners complain about the lurid way in which the religion is depicted in popular culture as a form of "black magic."

Intoxicating rituals open contact with the spirit world, allowing Voodoo priests and priestesses to seek assistance and healing.

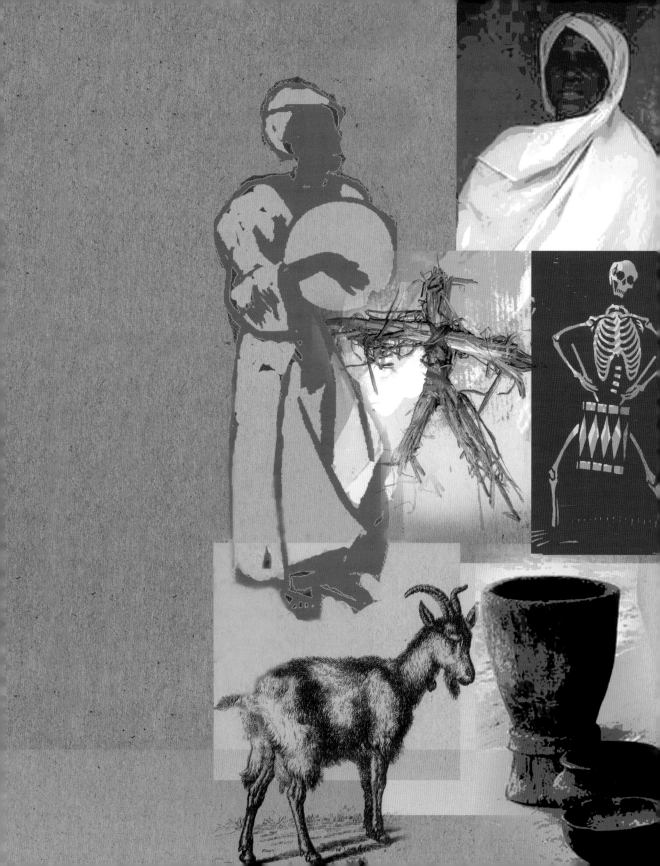

CANDOMBLÉ

the 30-second religion

Followers of Candomblé venerate

African deities, drawing on traditions from several parts of Africa (but primarily Yoruba) that were brought to Brazil by slaves. The deities are known as *orixás*, although there is some variation of nomenclature; there is a distant high God named Olorun, his son Oxalá, who created the world, and a small pantheon of other deities representing aspects of human experience and the natural order, such as war and agriculture (Ogum) and luxury and fertility (Oxum). Each person is the "child" of a particular *orixá*, and a follower of the religion (either a woman or a man) may choose to become an *iaô*, an initiate of a deity. Following the initiation process, the *iaô* represents the deity to the people, entering trance possessions and dancing, and after seven years the *iaô* may become a *mãe* or *pie de santo* (mother or father of saints). The gods are offered animal sacrifices, and they are consulted about problems through divination methods, such as throwing down cowry shells and interpreting the resulting pattern. Health and harmony depend on achieving a balance between the various forces represented by the different *orixás*.

3-SECOND SERMON
The gods give us life, protection, and advice, so we should reciprocate with food offerings, celebrations, and, in some cases, initiations.

3-MINUTE THEOLOGY
Candomblé has traditionally contained elements taken from Roman Catholicism, with the *orixás* identified with Jesus and the saints. Followers of Candomblé also typically describe themselves as Roman Catholics. However, since the 1980s there has been a movement to reject Catholic influence as a "syncretistic" imposition; those who take this view seek "re-Africanization" and advise the removal of Catholic images. However, some scholars believe that this quest for purity belies the historical complexities in the development of Candomblé.

RELATED RELIGIONS
See also
YORUBA
Page 14
VOODOO
Page 124

3-SECOND BIOGRAPHIES
IYA NASSO
fl.1830s

MÃE ANINHA
Eugênia Anna Santos
1879–1938

MÃE MENININHA
Maria Escolástica
da Conceição Nazaré
1894–1986

MÃE STELLA DE OXOSSI
Maria Stella
de Azevedo Santos
1925–

30-SECOND TEXT
Richard Bartholomew

With strong African associations, Candomblé followers look to the gods for security in return for offerings and veneration.

HARE KRISHNA MOVEMENT

the 30-second religion

The International Society for Krishna Consciousness (ISKCON) believes that the Hindu deity Krishna represents the supreme manifestation of God, and that he has been incarnated at various times in history, including as Rama and The Buddha. Most recently, he came as Chaitanya Mahaprabhu (1486–1533), who taught salvation through devotion (*bhakti*). ISKCON members express their love for Krishna by worship practices that include public dancing and preaching, and by repeating a 16-word mantra taken from the Hindu *Upanishads*, and which begins "Hare Krishna" ("Hare" refers to the energy of God). Through such activities the law of karma and the cycle of reincarnation will be overcome, although the ordinary devotee must remain under the guidance of a recognized guru within the movement, and moral precepts must be followed. The words of Krishna are believed to be recorded in the Bhagavad Gita, and adherents consider that the purest translation into English and most authoritative commentary was made by A. C. Bhaktivedanta Swami Prabhupada, who founded ISKCON in the United States in 1966. ISKCON is noted for providing free meals, both as a charitable act for the needy and to promote the virtues of vegetarianism, and for its mass distribution of literature.

3-SECOND SERMON
Sincere devotion to Krishna expressed through chanting, service, and right living will lead to God consciousness.

3-MINUTE THEOLOGY
Despite its conservative moral strictures and patriarchy, ISKCON's first appeal was to members of the 1960s counterculture, most famously George Harrison. However, following the death of Prabhupada, the organization experienced scandals involving gurus who were expelled for engaging in illicit sex and using drugs. While Prabhupada regarded the religion in universal terms, ISKCON today places greater stress on its Hindu background, and non-ISKCON Hindus are known to attend ISKCON temples for worship.

RELATED RELIGION
See also
HINDUISM
Page 32

3-SECOND BIOGRAPHIES
A. C. BHAKTIVEDANTA SWAMI PRABHUPADA
1896–1977

GEORGE HARRISON
1943–2001

RAVINDRA SVARUPA DASA
William H. Deadwyler
c.1946

30-SECOND TEXT
Richard Bartholomew

Adherents of the Hare Krishna movement worship Krishna as the Supreme Lord and aim to promote spirituality, peace, and unity.

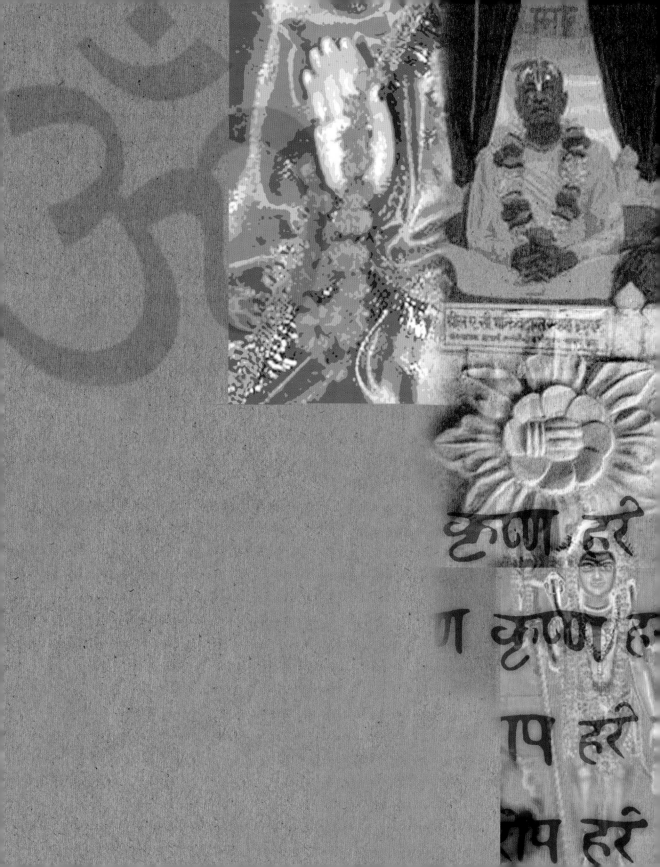

CHEONDOISM

the 30-second religion

Adherents believe that the Ruler of Heaven, Sangje, revealed himself to a young Korean scholar named Ch'oe Che'u in 1860. Sangje gave Ch'oe Che'u a cryptic phrase, which, when written on paper and swallowed, will cure disease and impart long life. Repeating the phrase in worship is believed to help humans to bring their thoughts and actions into harmony with heaven. In addition, humans should work to build a paradise on earth, and this has been understood to mean support for Korean nationalism. The teaching is characterized as "Eastern Learning" (*Tonghak*, the original name of the religion), in conscious opposition to "Western Learning" (*Sohak*), which was identified with Roman Catholicism. However, although the name "Sangje" comes from Chinese Taoism, the religion has a central prayer which uses the Roman Catholic term for God, "Chonju," and worship style and architecture suggest influence from Protestantism. The current name of the religion, adopted in 1905, means "Religion of the Heavenly Way."

3-SECOND SERMON
Humans and heaven are one, and humans can realize this truth by reverencing the Ruler of Heaven and repeating a sacred phrase.

3-MINUTE THEOLOGY
Cheondoism blends Chinese religion with Korean shamanism in the context of a nationalistic Korean identity. Ch'oe Che'u was executed for treason in 1864, and leaders of the group led insurrections against corrupt rulers in the 1890s. A later leader, Son Pyong-hui, helped to write the Korean Declaration of Independence, and in the 1960s members were prominent in patriotic pro-government rallies in South Korea.

RELATED RELIGIONS
See also
ANIMISM
Page 18
MAINSTREAM BUDDHISM
Page 36
TAOISM
Page 48

3-SECOND BIOGRAPHIES
CH'OE CHE'U
1824–1864

CH'OE SIHYONG
1827–1898

SON PYONG-HUI
1861–1922

30-SECOND TEXT
Richard Bartholomew

The repetition of a sacred phrase provided by the Ruler of Heaven will bring about harmony between heaven and earth.

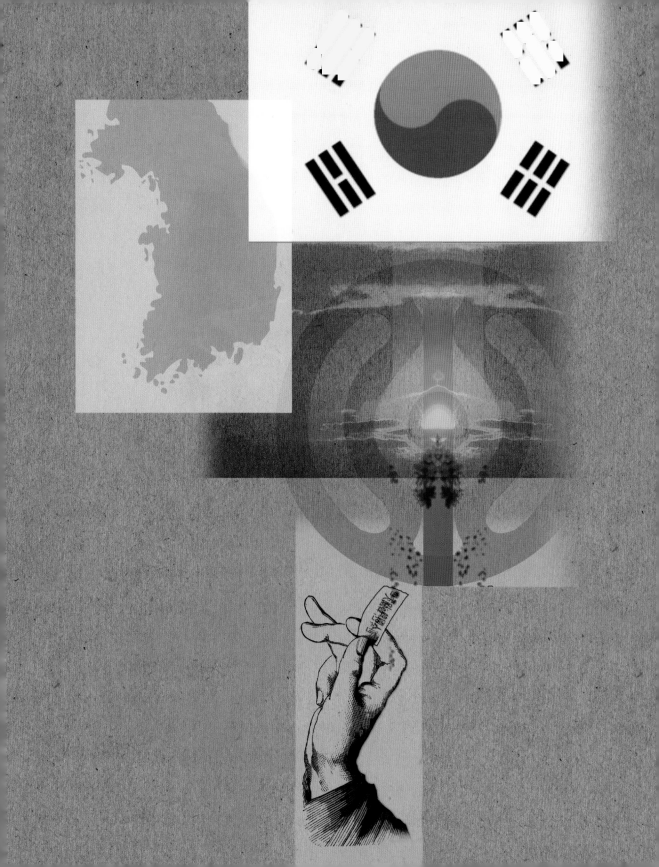

TENRIKYO

the 30-second religion

Followers of Tenrikyo believe

that from 1838 God the Parent (Tenri-O-no-mikoto) began to reveal himself through Nakayama Miki, a farmer's wife who was declared to be the Shrine of God and "Oyasama," meaning "Parent." God the Parent conveyed through Oyasama the promise that, following rebirths, humans will eventually experience an age in which everyone will enjoy the "joyous life;" suffering is due to causation (*innen*, or karmic fate). The path to the "joyous life" is to express gratitude for the life loaned to us by God, to understand that all people are brothers and sisters, and to detach ourselves from negative "dusts," such as envy or hate that settle in our minds and cause selfishness. Oyasama embodied the path by giving away her family's wealth and impoverishing herself. God the Parent later revealed that a location within the historical heartland of Japan is the center of the universe; this place, now within the city of Tenri in Nara, is where God the Parent resides, and it was here that humanity was created. Today, it is a place of pilgrimage, and it is venerated with sacred dance. Oyasama's male descendants now lead the religion.

3-SECOND SERMON
God the Parent wants all humans to partake of the "joyous life" through moral cultivation.

3-MINUTE THEOLOGY
Tenrikyo draws on folk shamanism and Buddhism, and despite the emphasis on Japan as the center of the universe, the religion regards itself as having a message for the whole world. However, it also shares elements with Shinto, and from 1908 to 1970 it was formally assimilated by the state into a form of Shinto. During her lifetime, Oyasama's message of equality and her female leadership were regarded with suspicion as well as hostility by the Japanese authorities.

RELATED RELIGIONS
See also
MAHAYANA BUDDHISM
Page 40
SHINTO
Page 54
SHINSHUKYO
Page 150

3-SECOND BIOGRAPHIES
NAKAYAMA MIKI
1798–1887

IBURI IZO
1833–1907

30-SECOND TEXT
Richard Bartholomew

Echoing the Buddhist belief in reincarnation, Tenrikyo teaches that attainment of the "joyous life" is achieved by denying negative tendencies.

天理市

NEW RELIGIONS

Babylon The most important city in ancient Mesopotamia, located on the Euphrates River, 50 miles (80 km) south of Baghdad. It was the capital of the Babylonian Empire from 612 BCE. To Rastafarians, Babylon is a symbol of the oppression of blacks by whites, just as the Jews were oppressed during the Persian rule of Babylon in 538–332 BCE.

black supremacy The belief that black people are superior to other races. At its most extreme, it is a racist ideology that encourages hatred toward anyone not of African ancestry, especially whites and Jews. However, some historians suggest that black supremacy is simply a reaction to white racism. Key organizations in the promotion of black supremacy are the Nation of Islam, formed in 1930, and the Black Panther Party, formed in 1966.

divine eye The symbol of the Cao Dai religion; a left-hand eye inside a circle or triangle. The eye is supposed to remind followers that the Supreme Being is "all seeing" and "all knowing" and that their every action is being watched. The left eye is shown because left represents yang, or the holy spirit, which watches over humankind.

dreadlocks Hair that is grown long, is twisted, and then becomes matted into long coils that look like rope. Although also practiced by other religions, dreadlocks are particularly associated with Rastafarians, who wear "dreads" as an expression of religious belief and to assert their black identity. Several passages from the Bible are quoted to support the practice, including Leviticus 21:5 and Numbers 6:5.

livity The Rastafarian way of life. This includes rejecting Babylon, or the modern way of life, by not paying taxes, only eating additive-free food, avoiding alcohol and coffee, smoking cannabis, eating a mainly vegetarian diet—or at very least not eating pork and shellfish—and growing hair into dreadlocks. The Rastafarian ethos has been criticized for its negative attitude to women and homosexuals.

Lucifer The word "Lucifer" is derived from the Latin *lux* (light) and *ferre* (to bear), meaning the light bearer, and original referred to the morning star. The term was used in the New Testament to refer to a Babylonian king who fell from power (Isaiah 14:3–20) and only later was the name applied to the devil. Nowadays, the word is used almost interchangeably with Satan, the devil, and Beelzebub.

Messiah The savior of the Jews, whose arrival is anticipated in the Old Testament. For Christians, Jesus of Nazareth fulfilled the prophecies and became their Messiah. More generally, the term is used to refer to any savior figure. From the Hebrew word *masiah*, meaning "anointed one."

Operating Thetan According to Scientology, the spiritual rank above "Clear." Once humans have been audited, they reach a state of "Clear." After that, further study will enable them to become Operating Thetans. There are many stages thereafter, with OTI-VII being preliminary stages before becoming a fully fledged OT at OTVIII, when the full truth is revealed.

qigong A Chinese martial art that combines meditation and movement. The full technique includes 460 movements, which involve visualizations and breathing exercises. Originating in China in 1122 BCE, the aim is to harmonize mind and body. From the Chinese *qi* or *chi* (energy) and *gong* (cultivation).

reincarnation Similar to the Buddhist concept of rebirth, except it is applied to a specific individual soul, instead of the more general concept of an "evolving consciousness." This idea is central to most Eastern religions, including Hinduism, Jainism, and Sikhism.

Supreme Being God, in the Cao Dai religion. The term is used to avoid any gender, race, or religious associations, although it is explicitly the same god worshipped by all other religions. The aim of the Cao Dai is to unite all believers in a supreme being.

syncretism The merging of different faiths, usually implying a successful new fusion. Christian Spiritualism is one example. The Baha'i Faith, which accepts Muhammad, Jesus, Moses, Buddha, Zoroaster, and Abraham as prophets, is considered another, although it has its own prophet, Bahá'u'lláh, and its own holy scriptures.

Thetan According to Scientology, the essence of life, similar to the soul in other religions. Thetans were self-willed into existence trillions of years ago and created the physical world for their own amusement. However, in time they forgot their true nature and became locked in their physical bodies. The aim of Scientology is to return them to their original state of "self-determinism."

Zion Originally a hill in Jerusalem conquered by David, but also a general term for a promised land. For Rastafarians, Zion is located in Ethiopia.

JOHN FRUM MOVEMENT
the 30-second religion

Believers regard John Frum as
God; he is thought to divide his time between America and Yasur, a volcano on the island of Tanna in Vanuatu, in the South Pacific. He first made himself known to local inhabitants in the 1930s through a vision, urging the rejection of Christianity and colonial currency, and a return to *kastom*—traditional culture. These were the customs and traditions that missionaries had forbidden, such as drinking an intoxicant called *kava*. Followers believe that subsequent events vindicated their faith: World War II brought sailors dressed in white to the island, along with technological marvels. Although these Americans left after the war, John Frum will one day return with a bounty of cargo from the United States. Believers offer prayers to Frum, and each year celebrate John Frum Day; ceremonies include raising U.S. flags and marching in mock U.S. uniforms, and replica chain saws are swung symbolically to prepare space for the building of factories. Members of the movement have also constructed an airstrip with bamboo control towers to facilitate the arrival of the cargo.

3-SECOND SERMON
John Frum is King of America, and he will make the island of Tanna into a utopia by restoring traditional customs and bringing cargo.

3-MINUTE THEOLOGY
The John Frum Movement is categorized as a "cargo cult." However, followers are not just motivated by a desire for material goods: the movement began as a protest against colonial domination. The movement's relationship with authorities in Vanuatu is tense. Paradoxically, it defends *kastom* by appropriating symbols of technology and of the United States, and it rejects Christianity while adapting millenarian Christian beliefs about a coming New World.

3-SECOND BIOGRAPHIES
NAMBAS
fl.1950s

NAKOMAHA
fl.1950s

ISAAK WAN
Current

FRED NESSE
Current

30-SECOND TEXT
Richard Bartholomew

Followers believe that John Frum, King of America, will return, bringing wealth and the reestablishment of traditional customs.

FALUN GONG
the 30-second religion

Falun Gong is based on the teachings of Li Hongzhi, a former musician who is regarded by followers as a master of qigong, a form of Chinese meditation and exercise used for healing and for increasing human potential. Li draws on popular Buddhism and Taoism, and he relates health to karma, in which actions in one's past lives affect one's current life. Karma is a black substance inside the body, which, through suffering or practice alongside moral living, can be made white. Followers should read Li's writings, get rid of "attachments," and follow the exercises that he prescribes; practitioners may develop paranormal powers, and Li claims to have a greater understanding of the universe than can be known by science. This includes the knowledge that aliens exist, and that the world has been destroyed and recreated a number of times and is about to undergo this process again. A sign that this is about to occur is the repression that followers have experienced in China since 1999; Li says that those who suffer or die for their belief will receive instant enlightenment. Members have held silent protests in Beijing and outside Chinese embassies abroad.

RELATED RELIGIONS
See also
MAINSTREAM BUDDHISM
Page 36
TAOISM
Page 48

3-SECOND BIOGRAPHY
LI HONGZHI
1952–

30-SECOND TEXT
Richard Bartholomew

3-SECOND SERMON
Certain exercises will transform the body and reveal a person's place in the universe; a new world cycle of destruction and renewal is imminent.

3-MINUTE THEOLOGY
In the People's Republic of China, Falun Gong is regarded as a "heretical cult" that exploits members, causes deaths, and is a threat to society. Practitioners have been detained and sent to labor camps, although claims of organ harvesting reported in Falun Gong media, such as the *Epoch Times,* are unsubstantiated. In 2001, Li was awarded a prize by Freedom House, a prominent American human rights organization, as a "defender of religious rights."

Adherents of Falun Gong seek enlightenment through the practice of qigong and the teachings of Li Hongzhi.

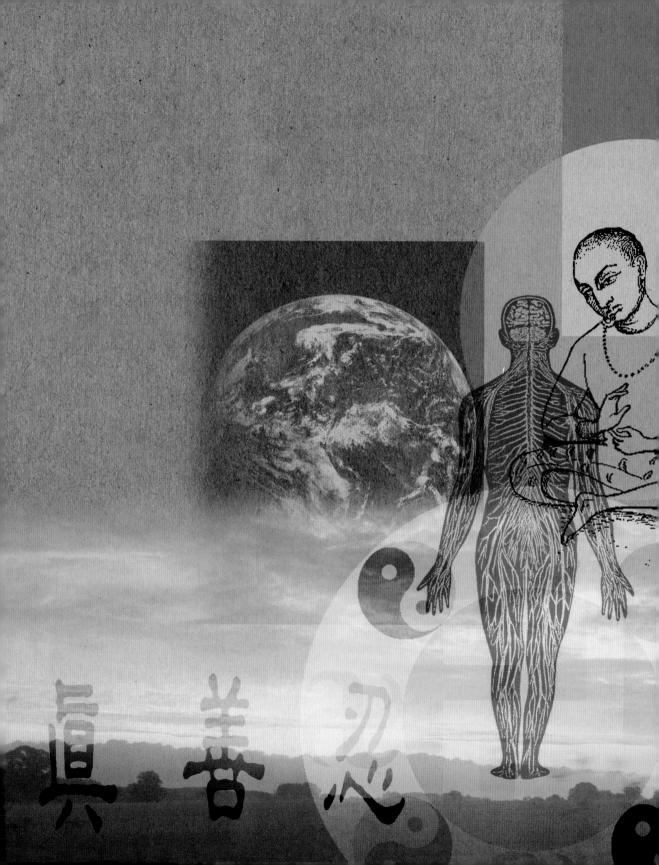

UNIFICATION CHURCH

the 30-second religion

Unificationists believe that God's plan is for his love to be made manifest through a perfect trinity of God, man, and woman, expressed through the "ideal family." However, the bond between humans and God was broken when Eve, the first woman, had intercourse with the angel Lucifer, and then with the first man. Jesus came to restore the trinity by having a family, but he was crucified before he could complete his work. Sun Myung Moon (born in Korea in 1920) claims to be the Messiah come again as the "True Father," while his wife is the "True Mother." Adherents believe that their bond with God is restored through taking part in a mass wedding ceremony performed by Moon, with a partner chosen by the Church. As a sign that humanity is one family, many Unificationist couples are international or interracial and Moon teaches that their children will be without the Original Sin inherited from Adam and Eve. Moon warns that the human sexual organs are precious and must be used properly; "free love" and homosexuality should disappear. Such teachings are called the "Divine Principle." Moon does not believe he is God and believers object to being called "Moonies."

3-SECOND SERMON
The perfect marriage of the Messiah restores humanity's bond with God; Rev. Moon is the "True Father" who completes the work of Jesus.

3-MINUTE THEOLOGY
Although the theology of the Unification Church diverges from traditional Christianity, Moon was raised as a Presbyterian and he regards his theology as Christian. Organizations founded by the church promote interfaith activities and Moon's emphasis on marriage has attracted some African Catholic clerics whose own church demands that priests be celibate. Moon's parents had formerly been Confucians before they became Christians, and the scholar Ninian Smart described Moon's teachings as "Evangelical Confucianism."

RELATED RELIGIONS
See also
CONFUCIANISM
Page 50
CALVINISM
Page 90

3-SECOND BIOGRAPHIES
SUN MYUNG MOON
"True Father"
1920–

HAK JA HAN MOON
"True Mother"
1943–

HYO JIN MOON
1962–2008

HYUN JIN (PRESTON) MOON
1969–

30-SECOND TEXT
Richard Bartholomew

Mass wedding ceremonies symbolize the reunification between God, man, and woman—the perfect trinity.

CAO DAI

the 30-second religion

Cao Dai was established in southern Vietnam in 1926. It teaches that the religious founders and other great figures of the past represent two earlier eras of divine communication with the world. The Third Era was revealed to a Vietnamese civil servant named Ngo Minh Chieu, when he was contacted by a spirit named Cao Dai during a séance; the name means "Roofless Tower," and refers to the "Supreme Being." Believers also adhere to further teachings delivered through mediums, both directly from Cao Dai and through various disembodied spirits of the dead. One such spirit is that of the French author Victor Hugo, who is thought to have been the Supreme Being's messenger to the West. Clergy are divided into three subgroups representing Buddhism, Confucianism, and Taoism, and organized along a structure borrowed from Roman Catholicism (although there is no Pope at present, and women are allowed some positions). The Supreme Being is symbolized as a left eye, called the Celestial Eye, and significant figures such as The Buddha and Jesus are among a group of deities at levels below Cao Dai. Adherents believe in karma, and seek merit through religious practice and service to society to escape the cycle of reincarnation.

3-SECOND SERMON
This is the Third Era of Salvation; religions are united in the worship of the Supreme Being, and there is communication with the spirit world.

3-MINUTE THEOLOGY
Cao Dai represents a modernizing synthesis that began by appealing to educated Vietnamese living under colonial rule; this modern perspective includes the emphasis on spirit contact, since Western spiritualist phenomena have been regarded in some circles as scientific. Cao Dai is also associated with anticolonialism, and festivals and exhibitions organized by the religion have celebrated progress and spiritual evolution by showing members in modern professions.

RELATED RELIGIONS
See also
MAINSTREAM BUDDHISM
Page 36
TAOISM
Page 48
CONFUCIANISM
Page 50
SPIRITUALISM
Page 122

3-SECOND BIOGRAPHIES
LE VAN TRUNG
1875–1934

NGO MINH CHIEU
1878–1932

PHAM CONG TAC
1890–1959

30-SECOND TEXT
Richard Bartholomew

Utilizing elements of Buddhism, Cao Dai, through the teachings of the eponymous Supreme Being, will lead followers to break the cycle of reincarnation.

SCIENTOLOGY
the 30-second religion

According to L. Ron Hubbard's
book *Dianetics* (1950), humans are limited by "engrams," bad experiences stored in the unconscious mind that affect behavior. These experiences may be from earlier in one's life, from the womb, or from past lives. Engrams can be removed through a process called "auditing"—this involves answering questions, either using the book or in a professional environment while attached to a device invented by Hubbard called the E-Meter. Psychiatry, by contrast, is rejected as harmful, particularly in its use of drugs. Those who have completed the process are called "Clears." Hubbard's subsequent teaching states that a "Clear" can further develop the inner self, called a "Thetan." A Scientologist seeks to become an Operating Thetan (OT), and then to pass through various levels. At OT III, a Scientologist learns about how the Thetans were brought to the earth by Xenu, a galactic dictator, in traumatic circumstances 75 million years ago. However, this knowledge is believed to be dangerous to the unprepared, and it will be meaningful only if revealed in a ritual context. Hubbard discovered this through scientific investigation, not through revelation, although some Scientologists regard the story as allegorical. Hubbard is venerated as the greatest author, inventor, and explorer.

3-SECOND SERMON
Human functioning and awareness can be dramatically improved, and with progress comes personal development from secret knowledge about the history of the universe.

3-MINUTE THEOLOGY
Hubbard is reported to have said in the 1940s that he would like to start a religion to make money, and skeptics allege that Scientology is not a real religion. The Church is known for having an aggressive attitude to critics, and in the 1970s it was beset with allegations of criminality in more than one country in pursuit of its interests. Recently, masked anti-Scientologist activists calling themselves "Anonymous" have picketed Scientologist establishments.

3-SECOND BIOGRAPHIES
L. RON HUBBARD
1911–1986

MARY SUE HUBBARD
1932–2002

MICHAEL MISCAVAGE
1960–

30-SECOND TEXT
Richard Bartholomew

Having divested yourself of bad engrams, as a "Clear" you can embark on a series of stages that will reveal the true history of the universe.

RASTAFARIAN MOVEMENT

the 30-second religion

The Rastafarian movement

began in Jamaica, when the coronation of Ras Tafari as Emperor Haile Selassie of Ethiopia in 1930 was interpreted as a prophetic event by some black Jamaicans. While the Caribbean and most of Africa were under white colonial domination, Ethiopia remained a proud and independent black African nation, and Haile Selassie, as God, would restore black supremacy and bring blacks back to Africa. The Bible, complemented by other texts, was interpreted in the light of the situation of blacks: just as the ancient empire of Babylon had oppressed the Jews, so whites were "Babylon" oppressing the black chosen people, considered reincarnated Israelites, and Ethiopia was Zion. Believers express their identity through the "livity," a way of life that emphasizes naturalness. Hair is worn as dreadlocks, diet is vegetarian, and herbal medicine is favored; in particular, ganja (marijuana) is regarded as a sacrament that brings spiritual healing when smoked. Language is adapted to convey Rastafarian experience: human dignity and subjectivity are expressed by using "I" instead of the Creole *mi* (me), and the divine essence inside each person is called "I and I."

3-SECOND SERMON
God redeems black people from white oppression, and he came to the earth as Haile Selassie, the Emperor of Ethiopia.

3-MINUTE THEOLOGY
The figure of Haile Selassie (who died in 1975) is no longer central for many Rastafarians, and the idea of a return to Africa is often understood symbolically in terms of self-expression within white-majority societies. Personal liberation not black supremacy is stressed, and there are now also white Rastafarians. However, despite the emphasis on liberation, the religion remains patriarchal, and Rasta women have complained about their subordinate position within the religion.

3-SECOND BIOGRAPHIES
HAILE SELASSIE
1892–1975

JOSEPH HIBBERT
1894–date unknown

MARCUS GARVEY
1887–1940

LEONARD PERCIVAL HOWELL
1898–1981

ARCHIBALD DUNKLEY
fl.1930s

BOB MARLEY
1945–1981

30-SECOND TEXT
Richard Bartholomew

God, manifest as the Emperor Haile Selassie, arrived on the earth to help raise black consciousness.

SHINSHUKYO

the 30-second religion

Japanese religion is characterized by syncretism and decentralization: typically, a birth is marked by a Shinto ceremony and Buddhism provides funeral services. "Shinshukyo" refers to "Newly Rising Religions," although in fact many groups so described draw on various aspects of this diverse and ancient religious heritage as interpreted by a particular individual. These founders and religious leaders, for adherents, make religion relevant for today, and the organizations that promote their teachings have replaced older patterns of religious affiliation. Some leaders, following the shamanistic aspects of Japanese religion, are believed to be channeling messages directly from a god and to have supernatural powers, such as healing. Others are venerated as teachers of exceptional insight; a New Religion may have a founder of the first type who is succeeded by a leader of the second type. Japanese New Religions tend to focus on concerns in this world, particularly health and personal success. The most successful Japanese New Religion is Soka Gakkai; this group emphasizes the traditional Buddhist practice of chanting the sacred text of the *Lotus Sutra*, but it teaches that this will have concrete material as well as spiritual benefits. Some New Religions also assimilate ideas from Christianity or from popular culture.

RELATED RELIGIONS
See also
MAHAYANA BUDDHISM
Page 40
SHINTO
Page 54
TENRIKYO
Page 132

3-SECOND BIOGRAPHIES
NAKAYAMA MIKI
1798–1887

KAWATE BUNJIRO
1814–1883

DEGUCHI NAO
1836–1918

DAISAKU IKEDA
1928–

SHOKO ASAHARA
1955–

30-SECOND TEXT
Richard Bartholomew

The New Religions of Japan are grounded in Buddhism and Shinto, but reinterpreted for a modern Japan by influential leaders.

3-SECOND SERMON
Religion in Japan is renewed and made relevant through the revelations and insights of founders and teachers.

3-MINUTE THEOLOGY
New Religions often face suspicion or ridicule from wider society, and media reports on Japanese New Religions have often focused on particularly eccentric groups with leaders who, to outside observers, appear to be dishonest or deluded. There has been less tolerance for New Religions in Japan since the Tokyo terrorist attack of 1995, when Aum Shinrikyo unleashed poison gas on the public as a result of its beliefs about the end of the world.

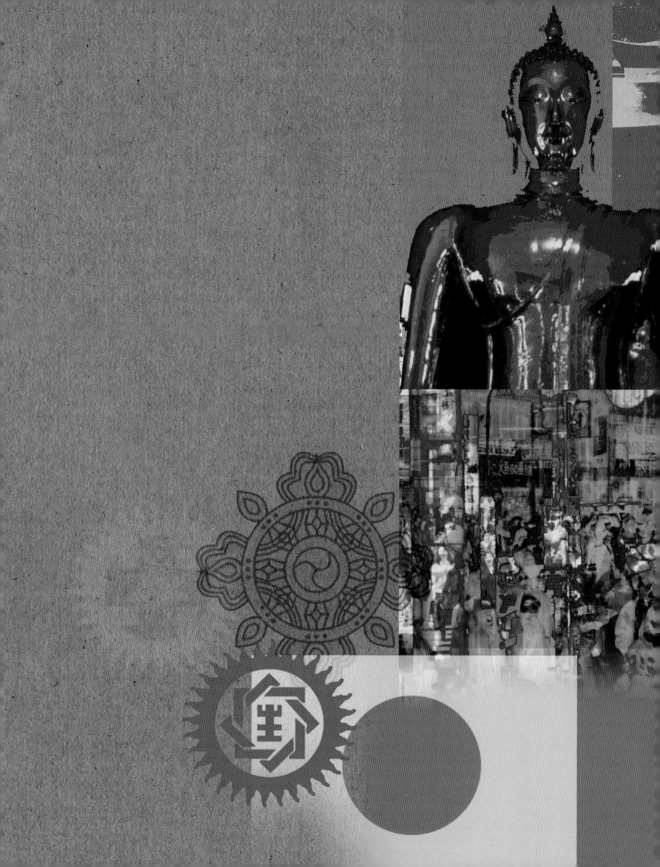

APPENDICES

RESOURCES

BOOKS

Animism: Respecting the Living World
Graham Harvey
(Columbia University Press, 2005)

A Brief Introduction to Hinduism
A. L. Herman
(Westview Press, 1991)

Buddhist Religions: A Historical Introduction
Richard H. Robinson, Willard L. Johnson, and Thanissaro Bhikkhu
(Wadsworth, 2004)

Christian Theology. An Introduction
Alister E. McGrath
(Wiley-Blackwell, 2010)

Contemporary Paganism: Listening People, Speaking Earth
Graham Harvey
(NYU Press, 2000)

Encountering Religion: An Introduction to the Religions of the World
Ian Markham and Tinu Ruparell (eds)
(Wiley-Blackwell, 2001)

Historical Dictionary of Shamanism
Graham Harvey and Robert J. Wallis
(The Scarecrow Press Inc., 2007)

Judaism
Nicholas de Lange
(Oxford University Press, 2003)

Magic and the Millennium: A Sociological Study of Religious Movements of Protest among Tribal and Third-World Peoples
Bryan R. Wilson
(Harper & Row, 1973)

The New Believers: A Survey of Sects, Cults and Alternative Religions
David V. Barrett
(Cassell, 2001)

A New Dictionary of Religions
John R. Hinnells (ed.)
(Wiley-Blackwell, 1995)

New Religions: A Guide—New Religious Movements, Sects and Alternative Spiritualities
Christopher Partridge and J. Gordon Melton
(Oxford University Press, 2004)

The Oxford Handbook of New Religious Movements
James R. Lewis
(Oxford University Press, 2008)

Religion in China
Richard C. Bush
(Argus, 1978)

Religion in Contemporary Japan
Ian Reader
(University of Hawaii Press, 1991)

Religions in Focus: New Approaches to Tradition and Contemporary Practices
Graham Harvey (ed.)
(Equinox Publishing, 2009)

Religions in the Modern World
Linda Woodhead, Hiroko Kawanami,
and Christopher Partridge (eds)
(Routledge, 2009)

*Western Muslims and the
Future of Islam*
Tariq Ramadan
(Oxford University Press, 2005)

A World Religions Reader
Ian Markham and Christy Lohr (eds)
(Wiley-Blackwell, 2009)

MAGAZINES/JOURNALS

*International Journal for the Study
of New Religions*
http://www.equinoxjournals.com/IJSNR

*The Journal of the American
Academy of Religion*
http://jaar.oxfordjournals.org/

Journal of Contemporary Religion
http://www.tandf.co.uk/journals/cjcr

The Journal of Religion
http://www.journals.uchicago.edu

The Journal of Religion and Society
http://moses.creighton.edu/JRS/

Reviews in Religion and Theology
http://www.blackwellpublishing.com/
journal.asp

WEB SITES

ABC Online Religion and Ethics Portal
http://www.abc.net.au/religion/
Collection of articles, commentaries, and
interviews on religious and ethical subjects
hosted by Australian broadcaster ABC.

BBC Religion
http://www.bbc.co.uk/religion/
Portal to articles and links about religions
and religious subjects, hosted by British
broadcaster BBC.

CESNUR: Center for Studies on New Religions
http://www.cesnur.org/
An international network of associations of
scholars working in the field of new religious
movements.

*INFORM: Information Network Focus on
Religious Movements*
http://www.inform.ac/
An independent charity providing balanced,
up-to-date information about new and
alternative religions or spiritual movements.

Religion Online
http://www.religion-online.org
Collection of scholarly articles, mainly from a
Christian perspective.

The Religion Hub
http://www.thereligionhub.com/
Interactive social network for people
interested in religion.

NOTES ON CONTRIBUTORS

Richard Bartholomew has a Ph.D. from the School of Oriental and African Studies, University of London, UK and he has published articles on the subject of religion and media. He runs a blog on religion and current affairs, which can be found here: http://barthsnotes.wordpress.com/. He also compiles indexes for academic books on religion.

Mathew Guest is senior lecturer in the department of Theology and Religion at Durham University, UK. He teaches classes in the study of religion, religion in contemporary Britain, and religious innovations in the modern world, and his research focuses on the sociology of contemporary evangelical Christianity. He is the author and editor of five books, including *Bishops, Wives and Children: Spiritual Capital Across the Generations* (with Douglas Davies), *Congregational Studies in the UK: Christianity in a Post-Christian Context* (edited with Karin Tusting and Linda Woodhead), *Religion and Knowledge: Sociological Perspectives* (edited with Elisabeth Arweck) and *Evangelical Identity and Contemporary Culture: A Congregational Study in Innovation*.

Graham Harvey is Reader in Religious Studies at The Open University, UK, where he cochairs the M.A. in Religious Studies. His research is mostly concerned with contemporary indigenous people, especially in North America and Oceania, but also in diaspora. He has also published about Paganism. Much of his teaching-related work engages with Judaism, pilgrimage, and the performance of religion.

Russell Re Manning is an Affiliated Lecturer at the Faculty of Divinity and a Fellow of St. Edmund's College at the University of Cambridge, UK. His interests include philosophy of religion, theology and the arts, and the science-religion dialogue. His books include *The Oxford Handbook of Natural Theology* and *The Cambridge Companion to Paul Tillich*.

Alexander Studholme is Lecturer in Indian Religions at the School of Theology and Religious Studies at Bangor University in Wales. His interests include mantras, Jungian approaches to Buddhism, and the Wisdom Christianity of Bede Griffiths. He is a member of the Dzogchen Community of the Tibetan lama, Namkhai Norbu Rinpoche. He is the author of *The Origins of Om Manipadme Hum, A Study of the Karandavyuha Sutra*.

INDEX

A
Aboriginal dreaming 16–17
Ahmad, Mirza Ghulam 74
Ahmadiyya 74–75
Ali 68
Allah, Baha' 76, 119, 137
Anglicanism 92–93
Animism 18–19, 54

B
Baha'i Faith 76–77, 119
Baptist Christianity 110–11
Baptist World Alliance (BWA) 110
Bhagavad Gita 34–35, 118, 128
Bible, The 65, 86–87
Buddha, The 36, 144
Buddhism 36–41, 42, 132, 140, 144, 150
    Mahayana 39, 40–41, 48
    mainstream 24, 36–37
    Vajrayan (tantric) 39

C
Calvin, John 90
Calvinism 90–91
Candomblé 126–27
Cao Dai 144–45
Catholicism see Eastern Orthodoxy and Roman Catholicism
Cheondoism 130–31
Ch'oe Che'u 130
Christian Science 114–15
Chuang Tzu 48
Confucianism 24, 50–51, 53, 142, 144
Confucius 50
Coptic Christianity 102–3
credobaptism 100, 110

D
dharma 30, 32

E
Eastern Orthodoxy 72, 84–85, 118
Eddy, Mary Baker 114
Episcopalianism see Anglicanism
Eucharist 80, 82

F
Falun Gong 140–41
First Great Awakening 80, 94
Fox, George 96
Frum, John 138

G
Gandhi, Mohandas 42
al-Ghazali 72
Great Schism 81, 84
Guru Granth Sahib 46–47
    Adi Granth 44, 47

H
hadith 58, 66
halacha 58, 60
Hare Krishna movement 128–29
Henry VIII, King of England 92
Hinduism 32–33, 44, 118, 128
Hubbard, L. Ron 146

I
I Ching 52–53
International Society for Krishna Consciousness (ISKCON) 128
Islam 66–71
    Shi'a 68–69
    Sunni 66–67
Izo, Iburi 132

J
Jainsim 42–43
Jehovah's Witnesses 108–9

Jesus
Jesus Christ 82, 84, 88, 102, 106, 144
Jesus Christ of Latter-day Saints, Church of 106
John Frum movement 138–39
Judaism 60–63
    Hasidic Jews 58, 60
    Orthodox 60–61
    Reform 62–63
    Ultraorthodox Jews 60

K
karma 30, 32, 42, 128, 140
Krishna 35, 118, 128

L
Lao Tzu 48
Le Van Trung 144
Li Hongzhi 140
Luther, Martin 88, 90, 92
Lutheranism 88–89

M
Mahavira 42
Mary, mother of Jesus 82, 88
Mesoamerican religion 22–23

ACKNOWLEDGMENTS

PICTURE CREDITS
The publisher would like to thank the following
individuals and organizations for their kind
permission to reproduce the images in this book.
Every effort has been made to acknowledge the
pictures, however we apologize if there are any
unintentional omissions.

Alamy/Biju: 34; Imagebroker: 38; Doug Steley C.: 52.
Corbis/Reuters/Munish Sharma: 46.
iStockphoto/Karim Hesham: 70.